MAIN Squeeze

JUICING RECIPES FOR YOUR *healthiest* SELF

IRIS McCARTHY

MAIN
Squeeze

JUICING RECIPES FOR YOUR *healthiest* SELF

ISBN 13: 978-1-4621-1560-0

Published by Front Table Books, an imprint of Cedar Fort, Inc.
2373 W. 700 S., Springville, UT 84663
Distributed by Cedar Fort, Inc., www.cedarfort.com

Library of Congress Control Number: 2015933330

Cover design by Michelle May
Page design by M. Shaun McMurdie
Cover design © 2015 Lyle Mortimer
Edited by Justin Greer

Printed in China

10 9 8 7 6 5 4 3 2 1

Printed on acid-free paper

Acknowledgments & Special Thanks

To my mother and sister, who would both be tickled (but not surprised) to see where I've landed in my professional life.

It would be absolutely foolish of me to think that I have reached this point in my career without the assistance, guidance, and support of some amazingly talented people I've had the good fortune of encountering along the way. I will forever be grateful to my physician and nutritionist for encouraging me to embark on my journey to good health, to my friends who have willingly offered themselves as my "culinary guinea pigs" as I've tested countless juice recipes on their now-fatigued palates, and lastly to Tom Ciavarella, my literary agent, whose patience knows no bounds. Thank you, everyone—I raise a (juice) glass and toast you all.

I would also like to offer special thanks to the following companies who provided me with products, tools, and assistance in the creation of this book.

Vitamix—The blended recipes were created using the Vitamix Professional Series 300.

Williams-Sonoma—Many juices found in this book were created using a Breville Juicer Fountain Plus.

Emile Henry—Many juices found in this book were created using a Novis® Vita Juicer.

OXO—Airtight containers were provided for the purpose of storing produce.

ShopRite—The Kenny Family, owners of the Delaware locations of the grocery chain, provided produce for the purpose of recipe creation and testing.

Your sponsorship and support are greatly appreciated.

Disclaimer

Contents

Introduction

With our fast-paced, busy lives and constant subjection to environmental pollution and processed foods, it's no wonder that obesity, immune and digestive disorders, skin conditions, and food allergies have become prevalent. We live in a "too much" culture—too much salt, sugar, and fat have crept into our daily diet and placed an extraordinary burden on bodies that are not equipped or designed to handle the overload. In response, our bodies are literally breaking down as illness and disease rates continue to rise.

The good news is that we can turn the tide on much of what ails us with increased exercise, diet modification, and a return to clean eating. In general, the American diet varies drastically from what the body needs,

wants, or can handle; the average adult consumes 100 pounds of sugar and sweeteners a year—nearly 30 teaspoons a day.[†]

I've struggled with obesity all my life, and as I tried numerous fad diets and pored over countless self-help books, my weight ballooned. Nearly 3 years ago, I decided that enough was enough and it was time to make a change. I had no idea where to start until a friend mentioned juicing and I thought it couldn't hurt. After all, I'd tried just about everything else. I'll be honest, it took several tries and a major mental overhaul of the way I dealt with my food issues (can you say emotional eater?) before I began to see real change and, boy, what a change! Today, I am 125 pounds lighter and healthier and happier than I've ever been. Did I mention that clothes shopping is so much more fun now? (Come on, I'm a woman—I can't help myself.)

I figure if you've purchased this book you're probably interested in juicing, right? No matter how you approach the concept, adding fresh juice to your diet can provide wonderful health benefits; it is a great way to jumpstart your wellness routine. It is important that I mention that I do not advocate long-term juice fasts—mainly because they don't work. Why? Imagine spending 14, 21, or 30 days consuming nothing but juice. Sure, you'll feel great and you'll most likely lose weight, but once you begin eating solid foods again, you'll no doubt end up regaining any lost weight and having to go back to the drawing board.

For most of us, it's about taking baby steps and making consistent, small changes so as not to get overwhelmed. That's precisely why I love adding juice to my diet; it allows me to consume more fresh fruits and vegetables in an easy, uncomplicated way. Whether you're a novice or a juicing guru, I hope this book will be a helpful resource in your journey to great health.

†"The sweet life and what it costs us," Face the Facts USA, accessed December 21, 2012, http://www.facethefactsusa.org/facts/the-sweet-life-and-what-it-costs-us.

Juicing 101: The Basics

Chances are you're excited to start your juicing journey and you've already scoured the Internet and researched several pieces of equipment you think you'll need. I get it—taking control of your health is exhilarating—but before you drain your bank account, let's take a look at the essentials.

JUICER—There is a seemingly endless variety of juicers on the market and choosing one can be a daunting task. They range from inexpensive, basic machines to heavy-duty, commercial-grade powerhouses that are often found in juice bars, cafés, and restaurants. In its most basic form, a juicer can be as simple as a citrus press or a lemon reamer, but those won't give you the ability to create complex, multi-ingredient juices, so it is wise to invest in a quality juicer. The most common type of juicers on the market today are centrifugal extractors, which typically employ a fast-spinning blade against a fine mesh filter that allows the flesh of fruits and vegetables to be separated from the juice. The juice and pulp are then housed in separate containers. Though this is certainly the most popular type of juicer, serious juicing devotees tend to shy away from centrifugal extractors because the heat generated from their pulverizing can oxidize and destroy some of the produce's nutrients and essential enzymes, thereby rendering them a tad less nutritious than cold-pressed juices.

Cold-pressed juicers, also known as masticating juicers, are the latest types of machines to hit the juicing scene and are praised for their high juice yield. They work by first crushing and then pressing the fruits and vegetables. Because their mechanisms move slowly and don't generate as much heat as their centrifugal counterparts, they allow more of the fresh ingredients' essential nutrients to remain intact. Cold-press juicers also have the ability to process nuts, making them a favorite among those who like to make homemade nut milks.

BLENDER—There has been much debate as to whether or not a drink made from fruits and vegetables processed in a blender can truthfully be called a juice, and the answer really depends on what one considers juice. Technically, juice is the resulting liquid extracted from a fruit or vegetable. A blender does not extract juice; rather, it processes the whole ingredients together and does not separate pulp, fruit, or flesh. Some refer to this as whole-ingredient

juicing; others deem it blending and refer to the end result as a smoothie due to its pulpy texture and thickness. No matter what side of the debate you fall on, a blender is essential in the preparation of juices that require soft fruits like bananas—which are impossible to process through a traditional juicer—and the addition of ingredients like coconut water, protein powders, and the like. Just like when choosing a juicer, blender options are plentiful, but it is important to choose a quality machine that can easily liquidize ingredients and blend smoothly. Don't think of a blender as merely a juicer's sidekick—it can

Juicy Tip

Vitamix is often considered the ultimate powerhouse of blenders, and its line of sleek, high-powered machines has garnered a loyal following. The heavy-duty motors found in the blenders make this brand highly desirable in the juicing world; many of the models have various functional settings specifically designed for whole-ingredient blending. Visit their website at www.vitamix.com.

often be the main star and can work to process all of a juice's ingredients, and not just the softer ones that need to be incorporated after the initial extraction. It should be noted that if a blender is used, all produce must be peeled and cored with its seeds removed unless you plan on using a strainer after blending. If the resulting juice (or smoothie) is too thick, consider diluting it with water (mineral, spring, or coconut) or additional fruit juice.

Juicy Tip Often the brand of choice for amateurs and professionals alike, consumer products giant OXO offers several solutions for whole-ingredient, refrigerated storage. Visit their website at www. oxo.com.

FINE MESH STRAINER— The use of a strainer is typically not necessary when using a centrifugal extractor or cold-press juicer, as they both do a fine job of extracting as much liquid from the ingredients as possible and separating the pulp. However, when whole-ingredient blending, it may be necessary to strain the juice to its desired consistency; this is the preferred method for those who do not care for pulp.

STORAGE— Juices are at their nutritional best when served immediately; however, if storage is a must, juice can be stored in an airtight container in the refrigerator for up to 48 hours. Juice tends to separate if not consumed right away, so shake or stir before drinking. Most of us find eating healthier much easier to accomplish when we are able to grab and go, and chopping, cutting, and peeling produce ahead of time can save valuable time. When storing whole fruits and vegetables, it is best to store them in airtight containers in the refrigerator. Cold produce works best for juicing and eliminates the need for the addition of ice. Choose a clear airtight container, preferably with a lock-top, when looking for storage options; some brands offer vented, temperature-controlled containers specifically crafted for the storage of fruits and vegetables.

VEGETABLE BRUSH— When using a traditional juicer, fruits and vegetables do not need to be peeled, but they still require a good scrubbing (yes, even organic produce as well). Choose a sturdy one with good bristles to get the job done.

CUTTING BOARD, KNIFE, AND PEELER—Even though many juicers and blenders can handle whole fruits and vegetables, there will be times when cutting ingredients down to size will be necessary. A heavy, non-slip cutting board with rubber feet and a sharp, manageable knife are essential. If using a peeler, choose one with a comfortable ergonomic grip so as to avoid slippage.

FOOD BAGS—Though it's not necessary to line the pulp-catching container of a juicer, it makes clean-up much easier. Simply slip a plastic bag into the compartment and leave a bit of overhang for easy removal and disposal.

THE DIRTY DOZEN™ AND THE CLEAN FIFTEEN™†

The Environmental Working Group (EWG), a non-profit organization dedicated to protecting human health and the environment, recently released an updated list of what is known as the Dirty Dozen™—a list that ranks the twelve most pesticide-laden fruits and vegetables grown both domestically and abroad. The group analyzed pesticide residue data from the US Department of Agriculture and the Food and Drug Administration to compile and rank the list of these popular fruits and vegetables. It should be noted that a lower ranking means higher pesticide content. In contrast, the EWG also compiled a Clean Fifteen™ list that ranks the cleanest produce with the lowest traces of pesticides.

The list does not encourage the strict avoidance of certain produce, but it does prove to be a handy reference guide when shopping for ingredients. It may be best to purchase the organic versions of the fruits and vegetables that appear on the list.

Healthy juice begins with quality ingredients, and selecting high-quality produce is essential to the juicing process. Does that mean you have to head to your local specialty grocery store and buy only organic fruits and vegetables? Certainly not, but as a general rule of thumb, if the ingredients don't *look* good, they probably won't *taste* good, either. Wilted greens, mushy, bruised fruit, and less-than-vibrant vegetables are just as unappealing when juiced, so drink with your eyes first.

DIRTY DOZEN™	CLEAN FIFTEEN™
Apples	Avocados
Strawberries	Sweet Corn
Grapes	Pineapple
Celery	Cabbage
Peaches	Sweet Peas (frozen)
Spinach	Onions
Sweet Bell Peppers	Asparagus
Nectarines (imported)	Mangoes
Cucumbers	Papayas
Cherry Tomatoes	Kiwi
Snap Peas (imported)	Eggplant
Potatoes	Grapefruit
	Cantaloupe
	Cauliflower
	Sweet Potatoes

† The list names are registered trademarks of the Environmental Working Group (EWG).

SUPERFOODS: WHAT MAKES THEM SO SUPER?

First things first, the following list of superfoods is not exhaustive. There are many more foods that make up the list, but the ones found below are optimal for including in traditional juicing, whole-ingredient juicing, or blending. Now, on to the good stuff . . .

What is a superfood and why should you care?

A superfood is defined as a nutrient-rich food that is considered to be especially beneficial for health and well-being. As a general rule, you should try to incorporate as many superfoods into your diet as possible. In fact, many of us are eating superfoods daily and may not even know it!

1. Almonds—Healthy lifestyle addicts go nuts for these nuts, and rightfully so. Eaten daily, a handful of these humble little nuts may help guard against cardiovascular disease and type 2 diabetes; they can also help you shed unwanted pounds and boost your energy.

2. Apples—Apples are such an awesome superfood, they've earned their own saying. We've all heard how an apple a day keeps the doctor away, and it's true. This miracle fruit lowers cholesterol, promotes bone health, and is chock full of dietary fiber, which aids in providing a feeling of satiety—keeping you from reaching for a second helping.

3. Apricots—These vitamin-rich orange jewels are overflowing with beta carotene and lycopene and aid in preventing cardiovascular disease. They are also an excellent source of fiber, which is necessary for bowel motility and preventing digestive sluggishness.

4. Asparagus—Often overlooked in juicing, this is one vegetable that shouldn't be ignored. The thin green stalks are known to have anti-cancer properties and are loaded with antioxidants that inhibit the growth of carcinogens and eliminate free radicals. Asparagus is also a natural and healthy diuretic that helps to relieve abdominal bloating and swelling; it is also excellent in assisting in the body's waste removal function.

5. Avocados—Though they may be impossible to

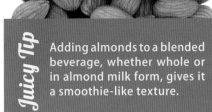

Juicy Tip

Adding almonds to a blended beverage, whether whole or in almond milk form, gives it a smoothie-like texture.

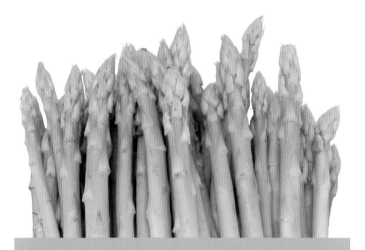

juice in typical juicers, a blender works very well in incorporating avocados into a variety of juices. Avocados may be the only fruit (yes, they're technically a fruit) that doesn't mind being called fat because they contain heart-healthy monounsaturated fat, also known as the good kind of fat. As if that's not enough, they help fight diabetes, reduce high cholesterol, and prevent certain cancers.

6. Bananas—Like avocados, bananas can't be processed in traditional juicers but can be incorporated into juices using a blender. Sweet and low in calories, bananas are a smart alternative to high-calorie, sugary snacks and are very filling. Favored by endurance athletes, bananas boast more than two times the amount of carbohydrates than apples and help provide stamina during exercise. The amino acid tryptophan, which aids in serotonin production, is found in bananas as well, and can help ease depression and anxiety.

7. Beets—If ever there was a vegetable that needed a good publicist, it would be the beet. Beets have earned the dubious honor of being one of the least favorite juicing ingredients due their earthy taste, but their health benefits cannot be debated. They are natural energy boosters and full of nutrients and antioxidants while remaining low in calories; consuming beets may aid in boosting immunity and guarding against certain types of cancer.

8. Bell Peppers—These vegetables may come in a rainbow of colors, but in terms of nutritional value, it doesn't matter which type you select because all varieties are great additions to a healthy diet. They are rich in vitamins B, E, and K as well as antioxidants, and even a small bell pepper has more than three times the recommended daily allowance of vitamin C.

9. Berries—When it comes to juicing, there is probably no more favored fruit than berries. If you want to win the war against rapid aging, try adding just one cup of berries to your daily diet. The compounds found in the antioxidants contained in berries can prevent the damage caused by free radicals.

Juicy Tip

Cruciferous vegetables belong to the family Brassicaceae (also called Cruciferae). Vegetables such as cauliflower, cabbage, bok choy, broccoli, Brussels sprouts, and similar green leafy vegetables are widely cultivated and take their secondary name, Cruciferae (Latin for "cross-bearing"), from the unique shape of their flowers, whose four petals resemble a cross.

A recent study shows that blueberries, the superhero of all the superfoods, may improve conditions like diabetes, excess weight, high blood pressure, tumor growth, and memory loss.

10. Broccoli—Most people don't think of juicing broccoli—it's often relegated to the far corner of the dinner plate as a side dish—but it can be a wonderful supplement to juices (especially of the green variety). As a member of the cruciferous family, broccoli may help lower your risk of getting cancer, and one serving has as much calcium as a glass of milk and more vitamin C than an orange.

11. Cabbage—As another member of the cruciferous family, cabbage is nutrient-dense and has been used for centuries by a number of cultures in the treatment of many types of conditions. It boosts overall health and may assist in dropping excess pounds; as a natural diuretic, it is helpful in eliminating excess fluid from the body.

12. Cantaloupe—This summer melon makes a refreshing, nutritious treat with only 60 calories per cup and zero grams of fat. Besides being packed with all sorts of nutrients, this is a fruit brimming with beta-Carotene, which makes dull skin glow and may help to prevent wrinkles and premature aging.

13. Carrots—Carrots have long enjoyed a reputation for being good for eye health; it's

not just some old wives' tale—it's true! These root veggies offer more than the recommended daily allowance of vitamin A in the form of beta-Carotene and are replete with filling fiber which keeps you feeling fuller longer.

14. Cherries—Don't ignore cherries when juicing just because pitting them can be a pain—the benefits they offer are well worth the effort. Tart cherries are known to conquer insomnia due to the significant amount of sleep-producing melatonin found in the crimson orbs. They also aid in the fight against high cholesterol, heart disease, and inflammation.

15. Grapes—These little, round free-radical fighters have been a favorite in many cultures all over the world and are brimming with

> **Juicy Tip**
> Using a pitter, a tool that uses a punching method to remove fruit pits, can be a lifesaver when dealing with cherries. They can be found in some grocery stores and specialty shops. Don' t have a pitter? Alternatively, cherries can be pitted with a pastry tip or a clean hairpin.

antioxidants. In addition to their sweet taste, grapes are great sources of vitamins B1 and B6, manganese, and potassium, which are considered building blocks of a strong and healthy body.

16. Kale—All hail kale! In recent years, that certainly has been the battle cry of health advocates everywhere; this cruciferous leafy green has been enjoying its time in the culinary spotlight, and though it can be used in a variety of applications, it is an excellent addition to a juicing regimen. Like many of its cruciferous counterparts, kale is rich in beta-Carotene and fiber and offers an abundance of phytochemicals—plant-produced compounds have been

> **Juicy Tip**
> Red and purple grapes get their deep, jewel-toned coloring from flavonoids—powerful antioxidants that are known for their ability to prevent blood clots and strengthen weakened tissue. Grapes also contain resveratrol, which, in recent studies, has been shown to guard against arterial damage and aid in the prevention of hypertension.

COMMON PHYTOCHEMICALS AND WHERE TO FIND THEM

PHYTOCHEMICAL NAME	BENEFITS	COMMONLY FOUND IN
Anthocyanidins	Blood vessel health	*Blackberries* *Blueberries* *Cranberries* *Plums* *Raspberries* *Red onions* *Red radishes* *Strawberries*
Beta-Carotene	Immune system Vision Skin health Bone health	*Apricots* *Broccoli* *Cantaloupe* *Carrots* *Collard greens* *Kale* *Pumpkin* *Spinach* *Sweet potato* *Winter squash*
Isoflavones	Breast cancer prevention Bone health Ease of joint inflammation Ease of menopause symptoms Lower cholesterol	*Soybeans*

PHYTOCHEMICAL NAME	BENEFITS	COMMONLY FOUND IN
Lutein	Eye health Heart health Cancer prevention	*Artichokes* *Broccoli* *Brussels sprouts* *Collard greens* *Kale* *Lettuces* *Spinach*
Lycopene	Heart health Prostate cancer prevention	*Pink grapefruit* *Red peppers* *Tomatoes* *Watermelon*
Resveratrol	Cancer prevention Heart health Lung health Ease of inflammation	*Grapes* *Peanuts*

Juicy Tip

Phytochemicals include a broad range of compounds produced by plants. They are found in fruits, vegetables, grains, beans, and a variety of other plants and offer many benefits to the body. Some common names for phytochemicals are antioxidants, polyphenols, flavonoids, phytonutrients, and carotenoids.

shown to fight cancer and cardiovascular disease. This nutrient-rich dynamo is full of antioxidants that combat inflammation and can detoxify a lethargic system.

17. Kiwi—This tiny tropical fruit is essential in the anti-aging fight; it is teeming with antioxidants and packs more vitamin C than an orange—the vitamin known for its immunity-boosting benefits and ability to prevent and combat everyday afflictions. Eat a small kiwi and you've just ingested folate, polyphenols, fiber, potassium, carotenoids, and a healthy dose of vitamin E (usually only found in nuts and oils). What a tasty way to get so many nutrients!

18. Lemons and Limes—Quite possibly the reigning kings of the detox world, these citrus fruits are an essential part of juicing. Their natural diuretic properties assist in flushing harmful toxins from the body, and their sour taste causes a puckering of the mouth, which promotes the production of bile—a bitter alkaline fluid necessary in the digestive process.

19. Mangoes—These tropical fruits have been a diet staple in Latin America for centuries; besides being juicy and delicious, they are a great supplement to your juicing routine. Like apples, mangoes contain loads of fiber, which helps to satiate hunger and keeps you feeling full. Potassium, vitamins A, C, and E, along with a slew of enzymes and antioxidants, are also found in these sweet treats and are helpful in the digestive process and guarding against colon, prostate, and breast cancers.

20. Oranges—Remember when Mom made you drink a glass of OJ when you came down with a cold? Known as one of the most popular citrus fruits, oranges are lauded for their immunity-boosting properties due to their high concentration of vitamin C. Their cancer- and heart disease–fighting ability makes them an excellent supplement to any juicing routine.

21. Papaya—Papaya does wonders for the body inside and out and is a perfect skin booster due to an array of antioxidants found in its pulpy yellow-orange flesh. Highly concentrated in vitamins C and E, the tropical wonder protects against cell oxidation, which can often lead to the hardening of arteries; papaya can also combat cardiovascular disease by improving blood flow to the heart and has been known to weaken cancerous cells by boosting the body's immune system and preventing them from spreading.

22. Peaches—The state of Georgia was spot-on in selecting the peach as the official state fruit. Excellent for promoting optimal eye health, peaches contain beta-Carotene and a host of nutrients that reduce the risk of macular degeneration, cataracts, and glaucoma. The fuzzy fruit also promotes good digestion and colon health thanks to its fiber content, and—listen up, beauty addicts—consuming peaches may allow you to toss out all your expensive skin creams and serums. They are packed with vitamin C and antioxidants, which keep skin youthful coagulation of the blood and swelling can be soothed by adding pineapple to your diet; studies have shown that certain types of tumor growth can be abated by therapeutic doses of bromelain.

24. Pumpkin—Did you know that you can juice pumpkin? Though it may not be the most conventional way to enjoy the squash, it can add both sweet and earthy flavors to a beverage. The antioxidants found in pumpkins can be a skin savior—they fight harmful free radicals that damage and attack healthy skin cells, which can lead to a number of health problems, including some cancers. You'll be smiling like a jack-o'-lantern after drinking pumpkin juice due to the L-tryptophan content—a chemical compound known for its depression-alleviating ability.

Juicy Tip

Feeling fatigued? Boost your vitality with pineapple—it contains manganese, a mineral that helps the body produce energy. Thiamine, also commonly known as vitamin B1, is found in pineapple and collaborates with other energy-producing enzymes to keep sluggishness at bay.

Although the highest concentration of bromelain is found in the stem and core of a pineapple, the enzyme is also found in the fibrous flesh.

and glowing—a much tastier alternative to slathering on a layer of cold chemical-laden cream, right?

23. Pineapple—This tropical fruit adds a familiar sweetness to any juice, and it's not only tasty but also packs a healthful punch. Bromelain, a protein-digesting enzyme, is found in the core and stem of pineapple, aids in the digestive process, and has inflammation-fighting properties. Excessive

25. Pomegranate—Once you get past the tough exterior and discard the bitter inner pith, you'll find the edible seeds, or arils, which have a sweet-tart taste. Pomegranates contain polyphenols, plant compounds that are indispensable in reducing the dangerous inflammation associated with cardiovascular

in spinach not only aid in keeping you energized throughout the day but also help keep your digestive tract healthy.

27. SPROUTS—Sure, they may look like grass clippings, but sprouts are insanely nutritious and packed with vitamins, minerals, fiber, and enzymes. Believe it or not, certain sprouts contain more protein than meat, and the amino acids they contain help make them easier to digest. Like many plants, sprouts contain chlorophyll, which is useful in cleansing and oxygenating the blood, making sprouts a great detoxifier.

• For hygiene's sake, wash your hands before handling seeds. You can use seeds, grains, nuts, or legumes in this process. For simplicity, these items will be

disease, and may lessen the thickness of arterial walls, allowing blood to flow more easily. Adding polyphenols to your diet, like those found in pomegranates, may help to stave off diseases caused by inflammation, like stroke, heart disease, and certain cancers.

26. SPINACH—He may have been a cartoon character, but Popeye knew what he was doing by eating his spinach. Besides its cancer-fighting properties, spinach is known to improve brain and cardiovascular function and strengthen bones. Eating spinach can literally make you smarter and stronger! The iron and fiber contained

Juicy Tip

Nothing deepens your understanding of your health than connecting to your food by actually growing it yourself. You can easily grow your own sprouts at home.

referred to as seeds throughout the instructions.

- Remove any broken or discolored seeds, stones, twigs, or hulls that may have found their way into your sprouting seeds.

- Place one type of seed in the jar. Use about a teaspoon of seeds or one-third cup of beans. Remember, they will grow in size during the soaking and sprouting process.

- Cover the seeds with pure water. If you are using a few tablespoons of seeds, cover with at least one cup of water. If you are using beans, nuts, or grains, use at least three times the water of the amount of seed. For example, one cup of water for one-third cup of mung beans.

- Allow the seeds to soak for 6 to 12 hours. It is easier to start them before, say, going to bed. They absorb the water overnight and are ready to start sprouting in the morning.

- Cover the jar with the sprouting lids or cheesecloth. If you're using cheesecloth, secure over the top of the jar with a rubber band. Drain off the water.

- Rinse thoroughly with fresh water and drain off the water again. Set upside down in a clean, cool spot in your kitchen area, preferably on a slight angle to allow excess water to drain off. Alternatively, use a stainless steel dish drying rack, which gives the sprout jars the perfect angle for draining.

- Rinse the sprouts a few times a day. Be sure to drain them well each time.

- Once the sprouts are ready to be harvested (this amount of time differs for each variety; alfalfa or mung bean sprouts are ready in about a week), place them in a large bowl of cool water, and stir them around to loosen hulls and skins from the seeds (this is an optional step). They'll usually come to the top so you can remove them. Don't worry about removing every hull. Doing so helps prevent spoilage so the sprouts will last longer. Drain sprouts well and store in the refrigerator, covered, for a week to 10 days, depending on the sprout type.

(Schoffro-Cook, Mary. "How to Grow Sprouts." *Care2* 6 April 2014. Web. 14 December 2014. http://www.care2.com/greenliving/grow-your-own-sprouts.html.)

28. SWEET POTATOES—Yes, sweet potatoes can be juiced, and they are delicious when incorporated in a beverage. Chock full of vitamins B6, C, and D, along with a healthy dose of beta-Carotene, the humble spud is one of nature's most nutritious vegetables. In fact, a small sweet potato contains more than three times the recommended daily allowance of vitamin A and a number of cancer-fighting phytochemicals.

29. SWISS CHARD—This leafy veggie comes in green and rainbow varieties and is quite the nutritional knockout. Low in calories, it's perfect for preventing weight gain, and the carotenoids (pigments) found within are helpful in promoting eye health. Swiss chard can help prevent the development of cataracts and may stave off degenerative retinal disease. Your heart will also thank you for consuming chard; the presence of vitamin K may help to ward off blood clots and clogged arteries.

30. TOMATOES—What is it that tomatoes can't do? The list of their health benefits is seemingly endless; they might very well be the perfect health food. They are low in calories, sodium, and cholesterol, but are best known for their hearty dose of the carotenoid

Juicy Tip

Stressed out? Find your Zen in sweet potatoes; the magnesium found in them is a mineral that is known for relaxing the body and mind.

lycopene—an efficient soldier in the war against cancer. Tomatoes provide the body with vitamins A, B6, C, and K, in addition to magnesium, phosphorus, copper, niacin, folate, and potassium; they are also free radical fighters and keep cell damage at bay.

JUICING TIPS & FAQS

Purchase the best quality produce available—It's true: juicing can be an expensive endeavor, and it's tempting to buy less-than-perfect produce from discount retailers, but do yourself (and your body) a favor and resist temptation. Instead, visit local farms, CSAs, and organic produce stands as they tend to offer higher-quality, nutrient-rich fruits and vegetables; buying smaller quantities also keeps costs down.

Don't buy in bulk—Buying large quantities of ingredients can be overwhelming—not only to your wallet but also to your refrigerator. Fresh juices are the best juices, and over-buying produce can lead to unnecessary spoilage and waste.

Resist the rainbow—Juicing can be exciting—mixing various fruits and vegetables and coming up with tasty concoctions can make you feel like some kind of cool mad scientist, but adding infinite ingredients to a juice is not always ideal. Not only does a bevy of fruits and veggies muddy the color

of a juice, it can also up the caloric and sugar content.

Give your produce a bath—Your produce needs to be washed thoroughly before juicing to remove harmful pesticides, waxes, and other chemicals. For produce with rinds and skins, use a vegetable brush to scrub them; for softer fruits like berries, fill a bowl with vegetable wash and give them a good swish—don't forget to rinse with cold water after washing. You can usually find vegetable wash in the produce section of specialty grocery stores, or you can easily make a batch at home.

Juicy Tip **DIY VEGETABLE WASH RECIPE**

Fill sink with clean water, add vinegar (3 parts water, 1 part vinegar) and 2 tablespoons of salt, and stir. Add fruit and vegetables and soak for 10 minutes. The water may be dirty and cloudy and the fruits and vegetables will be free of debris, wax, and chemicals. Remove produce from sink and rinse thoroughly with clean water.

If you prefer to make a vegetable wash in spray form, mix 1 cup of water with 1 tablespoon each of baking soda and fresh lemon juice. Pour mixture into a spray bottle (do this over the sink or a bowl as it tends to be fizzy) and shake gently to combine. Spray on fruits and vegetables and allow them to sit for 2-5 minutes before rinsing with cold water.

Frequently Asked Questions

Starting a new health regimen can be confusing and overwhelming—trust me, I know. If you're new to juicing, you probably have a ton of questions, and that's OK. Relax, resist the urge to run out and drain your bank account buying things you don't need, and let's talk about juicing.

Q: There are so many choices on the market. How do I choose the right juicer?

A: Juicing is quite popular these days, so it's no wonder that manufacturers are jumping onboard. There are many brands and types of juicers from which to choose, and your selection depends on what type of juice you want to make. Do you want cold-pressed juice, juice packed with the maximum amount of nutrients—or perhaps you plan on juicing mainly leafy greens? Well, you must take those things into consideration. There are several websites that provide an in-depth, detailed comparison of juicers and will help you in your decision making. One of the best comparison charts I've seen is one that can be found on the housewares site *Everything Kitchens* (www.everythingkitchens.com).

Q: Can I make juice in a blender?

A: Purchasing a juicer can be a hefty investment, and since many people already own a blender, whole-ingredient juicing (or blending) can be an easier endeavor. In comparison to traditional juicing, blending does allow for more nutrients, minerals, and vitamins to remain intact. Just remember that blending has its limitations and does not separate fruits and vegetables from their flesh, nor does it separate the pulp.

Q: How many juices should I consume daily?

A: Consuming 2–4 16-ounce juices per day, in conjunction with a clean, healthy diet, is recommended.

Q: The juices are not enough to keep me feeling full; I'm still hungry! What should I do?

A: There are a few ways to address lingering hunger. First, you can try adding more fiber-rich fruits and vegetables to your juice, as they will keep you satisfied longer. You can also drink more juice if the daily recommended 2–4 juices are not enough. Lastly, you can consume unlimited amounts of water, including coconut water, and unsweetened tea (as long as it's not the caffeinated black or green varieties) throughout the day.

Q: How long will my juice keep fresh?

A: Guess what? Real food spoils, and that's a good thing! Juicing can be time-consuming, and it's tempting to make a big batch to stow away for later, but you may want to reconsider. Fresh juice is at its best when served immediately because it tends to lose its nutritional value the longer it sits; however, it can be stored in the refrigerator in an airtight container for up to 2 days. Just remember, fresh juice has a tendency to separate, so it's a good idea to shake or stir it before drinking.

Q: I want to try a juicing regimen but I have to work. How can I do both?

A: You don't have to put your life on pause when beginning your juicing routine. You can make your juice ahead of time (see previous question), store it in the refrigerator in an airtight container, and pack it in an insulated bag or cooler (preferably with an ice pack) when you're ready to head to work. Make sure you keep the juice refrigerated or in an ice-filled cooler until you're ready to drink.

Q: Should I buy organic produce only?

A: Well, this is the million dollar question, isn't it? There are some juicing gurus who claim that organic is the only way to go, and while it is true that buying organic ensures that your produce is pesticide-free, it doesn't necessarily mean that non-organic produce is bad for you. All fruits and vegetables, including organic produce, should be washed or scrubbed thoroughly before juicing; if you don't want to commit to buying all organic produce, consider purchasing the organic versions of the Dirty Dozen™ (see page 9).

Q: What if I'm allergic to or don't like one of the ingredients in the juice recipe?

A: It's totally OK to substitute ingredients—that's the beauty of juicing. It's all about experimenting and finding what works for you. So, go ahead and unleash your inner mad scientist and feel free to tweak the recipes to suit your tastes.

Q: I turn into a monster without my daily coffee. Is it OK to drink coffee during my juicing regimen?

A: Sorry to burst your bubble, coffee lovers, but I need you to put the coffee mug down and back away slowly. Drinking coffee or any caffeinated products is not allowed while you're juicing. The whole point of adding clean, nutritious juices to your diet is to focus on your health and wellness and to cleanse your digestive system, and flooding your body with caffeine defeats the purpose.

Q: Can I add sweetener to my juice?

A: Juices, especially those made with fruit, tend to not need additional sweeteners, but if you find that your juice needs a bit of a boost, it's OK to add agave, honey, or another unrefined sweetener (I don't recommend using white sugar). It's always best to go the natural route, though. Start by using very ripe produce and chances are you'll get a sweeter, more palatable juice—adding oranges, carrots, pineapple, or other naturally sweet produce also ups the sweetness factor.

Q: I'm constipated. How do I get fiber while juicing?

A: Some people mistakenly report being constipated when juicing when it's really a lack of having fibers present in the body to digest. Juices are absorbed by the body, not digested, and without a lot of fibrous pulp, there's not a lot for the body to digest, which may mimic constipation. There are 2 types of fiber: soluble and insoluble. Soluble fiber breaks down in water and is passed through your system. Conversely, insoluble fiber is what remains in the pulp that is caught in the sieve of your juicer. Insoluble fiber is helpful because it bulks up stool and promotes regular bowel movements and a healthy digestive tract. If you're concerned about your fiber intake, you can adjust the settings on your juicer to catch less pulp or you can manually add the pulp back to your juice.

Q: I'm diabetic. Can I still juice?

A: People with diabetes must be cautious when drinking juices high in natural sugars as these sugars can cause blood glucose levels to rise. You should consult your physician or other healthcare provider before beginning any diet or program.

Q: I'm pregnant. Can I still juice?

A: Well, yes and no. Drinking a glass or two of juice daily while still maintaining a healthy, well-balanced diet is all right, but due to different nutritional needs, pregnant women should consult their physicians or other healthcare providers before beginning any diet or program.

Q: I heard that any juicing regimen that claims to detox your body is a scam. Is that true?

A: When it comes to juicing, there is much debate over the word "detox." I cannot vouch for others, but when I use the term "detox" I am referring to juice's ability to give your body's digestive system a break by not having to work so hard to process solid food. It allows the body a much-needed period of rest since juice is absorbed by the body rather than digested. Think of juicing like soaking a sponge in water; the sponge exerts little to no effort absorbing the water, right? Well, that's basically how juicing works. The truth of the matter is, your body's organs—namely the skin, liver, intestines, lungs, and kidneys—do a wonderful job of naturally detoxing your body. If those organs ever fail or become too dysfunctional to properly detox your body, there is likely no diet or regimen that will help.

Q: I just started my new juicing regimen and I have a killer headache. What's the deal?

A: Headaches are the not-so-nice part of juicing, and unfortunately it's common. It's normal to experience withdrawal-like symptoms as your body becomes accustomed to your new healthy lifestyle, especially if you've been on a steady diet of processed, refined foods.

Q: I've been juicing for a few days and I feel great! Can I keep going?

A: Congrats on feeling awesome! Doesn't it feel great to take control of your health and wellness? As I mentioned earlier, I don't advocate long-term, extended juice fasts, but I do support what I call "supplemental juicing," or adding juicing to a healthy, balanced nutritious diet and lifestyle. That means clean eating, consuming whole foods, and avoiding processed, refined foods and sugar. Adding 2–4 juices daily to a clean diet can drastically change your life and boost or restore your health.

Detox & Wellness

NOTE | Due to the variations in size of fruits and vegetables, recipe yields range from 8 to 16 ounces. All recipes use standard kitchen measuring cups and spoons; all spoon and cup measurements are level unless otherwise stated.

SUNRISE IN PARADISE

Rich in vitamin C, this blend of tropical fruits is the equivalent of drinking sunshine. In days past, sailors (and health-conscious pirates) were known to keep barrels of oranges onboard to eat in an effort to ward off scurvy, but you don't have to be a captain on the high seas to understand the importance of this vital vitamin. It has long been revered in the medical community as a natural remedy for ailments like the common cold, and it's known to boost immunity. Remember when Mom made you sip a big glass of OJ when you had the sniffles? She was on to something—this slightly kicked-up version packs a powerful punch of the good stuff, and the addition of echinacea makes it a wellness shot in a glass.

INGREDIENTS

2 oranges, peeled

1 mango, peeled, pitted, and cut into wedges

1 banana, peeled

½ cup coconut water (more if you'd like your juice thinner)

10–12 drops of echinacea, optional

PREPARATION

Juice the oranges and mango. If your juicer is not equipped to juice soft fruits, use a blender to process banana and juice together. Stir in coconut water and add drops of echinacea (if using); serve immediately.

• Echinacea, a derivative of the daisy, is praised not only for its cold-fighting benefits but also for its ability to kickstart the body's immune cells, making them more efficient at attacking abnormal cells, bacteria and viruses, and even cancer cells.

GET UP AND GO-GO

Everyday life, stress, and even the process of digestion itself can overburden the body—throw in a modern-day diet of processed foods and the overconsumption of sugar, fat, and animal products like meat and dairy, and it's no wonder that our bodies often suffer from lethargy and fatigue. The humble lemon is perhaps one of the best natural detoxifiers on the planet, and its ability to support healthy digestion and elimination makes it a frequent ingredient in detox recipes, while turmeric is regarded as nature's answer to commercial pharmaceuticals due to its anti-inflammatory properties. The warming effect of ginger and cayenne increases metabolism, stimulates circulation, and aids in the excretion of toxins—perfect for jumpstarting a sluggish system.

INGREDIENTS

2 lemons, peeled, pith removed

½-inch knob of fresh ginger

2-inch piece of turmeric

1 tsp. mānuka honey

6–8 drops of echinacea

cayenne pepper to taste (optional)

PREPARATION

Juice the lemons, ginger, and turmeric; stir in honey. Add the drops of echinacea and a few dashes of cayenne pepper, if using.

Juicy Fact

• Did you know the tart taste of lemons serves as a wake-up call to your taste buds and promotes bile flow to aid in the digestive process? So pucker up!

• The use of turmeric as a culinary spice dates back more than 4,000 years, when it was used in India in various dishes. Centuries later, explorer Marco Polo marveled at the way the unique cousin of the ginger root could be used in similar ways to saffron.

• Mānuka honey is a monofloral honey, meaning it gets its distinct flavor primarily from the nectar of one plant. The high-viscosity honey is produced in New Zealand and Australia and is the result of honeybees who feed on the mānuka or tea tree.

KICKSTARTER COOLER

Juicing newbies may shy away from this "garden in a glass," but the main "vegetables" in this detoxifying drink—tomatoes—are really fruit, so that knowledge may help in introducing novices to the world of juicing. In addition to being packed with essential vitamins A, C, and K, tomatoes are also an excellent source of potassium and folate—all necessary for a healthy, functioning body.

INGREDIENTS

2 tomatoes

½ cup broccoli florets

1 carrot

2 celery stalks, with leaves

¼ cup cilantro, stems intact

¼ tsp. cayenne pepper

ice

PREPARATION

Juice the first five ingredients. Stir in cayenne pepper. Pour into an ice–filled glass and garnish with the celery leaves.

Juicy Fact

• Lycopene, a bright red carotene and carotenoid pigment, is found in tomatoes and other crimson-colored fruits and vegetables, like watermelons, papayas, and red carrots.

• Early studies have shown that the consumption of tomatoes may lower cancer risk.

THE ELVIS PARSLEY

This whole-ingredient blended drink does not have the look of a traditional juice; the banana, nut butter, and almond milk give it a smoothie-like texture, but it's still a delicious way to detox thanks to pow-erhouse parsley. The addition of banana and nut butter gives this bevvy an almost indulgent feel, and because it is so filling, it's an excellent breakfast option.

INGREDIENTS

1 banana, peeled and cut into chunks

1 Tbsp. natural nut butter (almond, peanut, or similar)

¼ cup flat-leaf parsley

½ cup almond milk (more if you'd like your drink thinner)

2 tsp. agave nectar (optional)

ice

PREPARATION

In a blender, combine the banana, nut butter, parsley, almond milk, and agave nectar (if using). Process on medium speed until smooth. Pour into an ice–filled glass and drink immediately.

• Bananas are officially recognized by the FDA as being able to protect against heart attack and stroke and lower blood pressure.

• Gotta go? Bananas help relieve constipation by improving bowel motility. Going too much? Eat a banana to soothe the tract and restore electrolytes lost during diarrhea.

• Parsley, a powerful superfood, is bursting with vitamins, minerals, antioxidants, enzymes, and chlorophyll and aids in the detoxification of the liver and kidneys. It is also helpful in combating bad breath. It should be noted that pregnant women should not consume large quantities of parsley as it may cause unintentional pregnancy termination.

THE FRESH START

Ancient Romans understood the benefits of beetroot; they used it as a treatment for fevers and constipation. Not to be outdone by their neighbors to the West, ancient Greeks—specifically Hippocrates (the father of modern medicine)—often used beetroot in their medicinal treatments. Hippocrates advocated the use of beet leaves as a poultice for wounds. Beets get their color from a pigment called betalain, which is used as a therapy for a variety of conditions, including digestive disorders and blood diseases.

INGREDIENTS

1 medium beet, peeled and quartered

1 large cucumber

1 celery stalk

1 lemon, peeled, pith removed

2 small apples, quartered

1 cup loosely packed flat-leaf parsley

PREPARATION

Juice all of the ingredients and pour into a glass. Drink immediately.

• Beets stain everything—including countertops, utensils, and fingertips! When peeling beets, it's best to do so on a cutting board covered with butcher or parchment paper. Immediately rinse utensils and fingertips with warm soapy water.

• When juicing, always alternate between hard and soft fruits and vegetables so as not to clog the juicer.

COOL HAND CUKE

INGREDIENTS

2 medium cucumbers

4 celery stalks

½ cup loosely packed flat-leaf parsley

2 apples, quartered

1 lemon, peeled, pith removed

½-inch knob of fresh ginger

PREPARATION

Juice all of the ingredients and pour into a glass. Drink immediately.

COOL CITRUS BLITZ

INGREDIENTS

2 oranges, peeled

½ grapefruit, peeled, pith removed

1 lime, peeled

4 mint leaves

PREPARATION

Juice the first 3 ingredients and pour into a glass. Add the mint leaves and use a spoon to muddle them into the juice. Serve immediately.

Juicy Fact

• This juice tends to be frothy, so feel free to skim the foam off the top or allow it to settle a bit before drinking.

• Grapefruit can interact with or render certain medications ineffective, so check with your healthcare professional to get information about any contraindications.

RHUBARB RUSH

INGREDIENTS

1 lb. rhubarb, leaves removed

2 medium carrots

1 large orange, peeled

1 (1-inch) knob of fresh ginger

water, optional

PREPARATION

Juice all of the ingredients and pour into a tall glass. Add water if you find the consistency too thick.

Juicy Fact

• Rhubarb leaves are poisonous and must be removed before juicing the edible stalks. Use a sharp knife to slice leaves away from the center rib.

• Early spring is the optimal time to purchase rhubarb, as the rosy-colored stalks tend to be young and tender; avoid purchasing the vegetable later in the season when the stalks have turned green and become tough and acidic.

THE LEAN GREEN

INGREDIENTS

2 small bunches of
watercress

1 cup loosely packed
spinach leaves

2 Granny Smith (green)
apples, quartered

2 celery stalks, with leaves

PREPARATION

Juice all of the ingredients, making sure to alternate between the leafy greens and the apples so as to not clog the juicer. Pour into a glass and serve immediately.

• Due to the gritty sand that may be hidden in the leaves, spinach must be washed and rinsed thoroughly.

THE PRUNE EXPRESS

INGREDIENTS

4 large prunes, pitted

8 ounces water

1 apple

2 pears

PREPARATION

Soak the prunes in 8 ounces of boiling water for 30–60 minutes until they are soft and plump. Purée the prunes and water in a blender on medium speed; set aside and let cool. Juice the apple and pears and whisk or stir in the prune purée. Pour into a glass and serve immediately.

Juicy Fact

• Some prefer the warmth of the prune purée immediately after it is blended and like to add it to the juice right away. The warmth is especially soothing if you're experiencing digestive sluggishness or constipation, as it tends to assist in getting things moving.

Energy Boosters

EYE OPENER

INGREDIENTS

4 large carrots

½ cup loosely packed flat-leaf parsley

4 kale leaves, center rib removed

1 large apple

PREPARATION

Juice all of the ingredients, making sure to alternate between the leafy greens and the harder produce so as to not clog the juicer. Pour into a glass and serve immediately.

Energy Boosters

BERRY BLUSH

INGREDIENTS

2 apples, quartered

½ cup strawberries, plus extra for garnish

½ cup blueberries, plus extra for garnish

½ cup frozen cranberries, thawed

1 Tbsp. chia seeds

PREPARATION

Juice the first 4 ingredients and stir in chia seeds. Pour into a glass and serve immediately.

Juicy Fact

• Fresh cranberries are hard and can be tough to juice; it's best to purchase the frozen variety and allow them to thaw. The softened texture will make the cranberries easier to juice.

• Chia seeds are considered natural energy boosters—and rightfully so. They are a concentrated food containing healthy omega-3 fatty acids, carbohydrates, protein, fiber, antioxidants, and calcium. When added to a liquid, chia seeds expand, become gelatinous, and can act as a thickening agent. It can be off-putting to some, so it's wise to consume your juice immediately after adding the chia seeds.

PEACHY KEEN

INGREDIENTS

1 pink or ruby red grapefruit, peeled and halved, pith removed

1 large peach, pitted and halved

1 carrot

1 (½-inch) knob of fresh ginger

½ cup chilled water, optional

½ cup crushed ice

PREPARATION

Juice the first 4 ingredients and stir in chilled water (if using). Pour into an ice–filled glass and serve immediately.

GINGER ZINGER

INGREDIENTS

2 large carrots

4 tomatoes

½ lemon, peeled, pith removed

1 (1½-inch) knob of fresh ginger

½ cup crushed ice, optional

½ cup chilled water

PREPARATION

Juice the first 4 ingredients, pour into an ice–filled glass (if using ice), and stir in water. Drink immediately.

PURPLE PASSION

INGREDIENTS

2 beets, peeled and quartered

4 plums, pitted and quartered

1 cup seedless red grapes

½ cup chilled water

PREPARATION

Juice the first 3 ingredients, stir in water, and pour into a glass. Drink immediately.

- Beets stain everything—including countertops, utensils, and fingertips! When peeling beets, it's best to do so on a cutting board covered in butcher or parchment paper. Immediately rinse utensils and fingertips with warm soapy water.

WAKE-UP CALL

INGREDIENTS

3 blood oranges, peeled
(see "Juicy Fact" below)

2 plums, pitted and
quartered

1 cup raspberries, plus
extra for garnish

PREPARATION

Juice all of the ingredients, pour into a glass, and drink immediately.

Juicy Fact

• In many American grocery stores, blood oranges are not readily available. However, some specialty markets carry them, and they can even be ordered online from produce dealers. Blood oranges are typically in season from December to May, though the exact months depend on the variety.

THE GLOW GETTER

INGREDIENTS

1 small papaya, peeled, seeded, and roughly chopped

½ pink or ruby red grapefruit, peeled, pith removed

1 cup strawberries, plus extra for garnish

½ lime, peeled

PREPARATION

Juice all of the ingredients, pour into a glass, and drink immediately.

- There is no need to hull the strawberries when juicing.

APPLE JACK JUMPSTART

INGREDIENTS

4 apples, quartered

1 tsp. pure honey

¼ tsp. ground cinnamon

½ cup crushed ice

1 cinnamon stick, optional

PREPARATION

Juice the apples, stir in the honey and cinnamon, and pour into an ice–filled glass. If using, place the cinnamon stick in the glass and use as a stirrer. Drink immediately.

POPEYE PUNCH

INGREDIENTS

2 cups spinach leaves

2 Granny Smith (green) apples, quartered

1 kiwi

½ large cucumber

PREPARATION

Coarsely chop the spinach leaves if they are large. Juice all of the ingredients, pour into glass, and drink immediately.

UP-BEET TEMPO

INGREDIENTS

2 large carrots

1 medium beet, peeled and quartered

½ cup spinach leaves

1 (½-inch) knob of ginger

PREPARATION

Juice all of the ingredients, pour into a glass, and drink immediately.

Juicy Fact

• Beets stain everything—including counter-tops, utensils, and fingertips! When peeling beets, it's best to do so on a cutting board covered in butcher or parchment paper. Immediately rinse utensils and fingertips with warm soapy water.

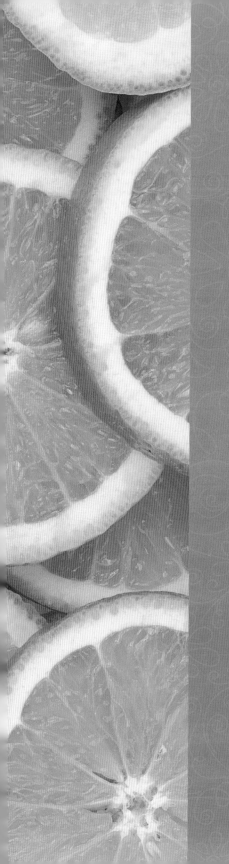

Soothers

TROPICAL TUMMY TAMER

INGREDIENTS

¼ large pineapple, peeled, cored, and quartered

1 yellow bell pepper

1 large kale leaf, center rib removed

cilantro to taste (¼ cup recommended)

½ cup coconut water

PREPARATION

Juice the first 4 ingredients, making sure to alternate between the leafy greens and the harder produce so as to not clog the juicer. Stir in the coconut water, pour into a glass, and drink immediately.

BERRY BERRY GOOD

INGREDIENTS

½ cup strawberries

½ cup raspberries

½ cup blueberries

½ cup blackberries

3 mint leaves

PREPARATION

Juice all of the berries and pour into a glass. Add the mint leaves and use a spoon to muddle them into the juice. Drink immediately.

GRAPE EXPECTATIONS

INGREDIENTS

1 cup seedless grapes, red or green variety

2 kiwifruits, peeled

2 apples

1 Tbsp. pomegranate seeds

PREPARATION

Juice the first 3 ingredients, pour into a glass, and stir in pomegranate seeds. Drink immediately.

CRANBERRY DELIGHT

INGREDIENTS

1½ cups frozen cranberries, thawed

1 large orange

½ cup plain Greek yogurt

2 tsp. pure honey

PREPARATION

Juice the cranberries and the orange. Add the juice, yogurt, and honey to a blender and process until smooth. Pour into a glass and drink immediately.

• Fresh cranberries are hard and can be tough to juice; it's best to purchase the frozen variety and allow them to thaw. The softened texture will make the cranberries easier to juice.

THE DEFENDER

INGREDIENTS

½ avocado, pitted, flesh scooped from the skin

1 large orange

1½ cups blueberries

½ cup chilled mineral water

PREPARATION

Juice the orange and blueberries. Add the juice, avocado, and water to a blender and process until smooth. Pour into a glass and drink immediately.

• To pit an avocado, slice in half lengthwise around the pit and then twist the two halves in opposite directions to separate. Hold the half with the pit in a kitchen towel and twist the knife to remove the pit—or, alternatively, hit the pit sharply with the knife blade so the knife is stuck in a pit and pull the pit out. Slice or dice the avocado in its skin with a paring knife and scoop out the flesh with a spoon.

SWEET TEA-LIEF

INGREDIENTS

1 green tea bag (or ginseng tea bag)

1 cup boiling water

2 Granny Smith (green) apples, quartered

2 cups spinach leaves

PREPARATION

Put the tea bag in a cup and pour the boiling water over it; let stand for 4–5 minutes. Remove the tea bag and set aside the liquid. Juice the apple and spinach and stir the juice into the tea. Drink immediately. (This juice can be served hot or cold.)

PEAR PICK-ME-UP

INGREDIENTS

3 pears, halved

3 oranges, peeled

1 (½-inch) knob of ginger

PREPARATION

Juice all of the ingredients, pour into a glass, and drink immediately.

- For a bit of added sweetness, 4–5 small pieces of crystallized ginger (found in the spice section of most grocery stores) can be used in place of the fresh ginger.

THE RELAXER

INGREDIENTS

½ small pineapple, peeled, cored, and quartered

½ cucumber

1 celery stalk, with leaves

PREPARATION

Juice all of the ingredients, pour into a glass, and drink immediately.

MELON CHILLER

INGREDIENTS

¼ honeydew, peeled and quartered

½ small watermelon, peeled and quartered

½ large lemon

1 basil leaf, shredded

crushed ice

PREPARATION

Juice all of the ingredients, pour into a glass, and drink immediately.

THE JOLLY GREEN

INGREDIENTS

½ honeydew, peeled and quartered

3 Granny Smith (green) apples, quartered

2 cup watercress

¼ cup flat-leaf parsley

4 large mint leaves

crushed ice

PREPARATION

Juice all of the ingredients, making sure to alternate between the leafy greens and the harder produce so as to not clog the juicer. Pour into a glass and drink immediately.

Skin Refreshers

CAROTENE CLEANSER

INGREDIENTS

4 large carrots

2 oranges, peeled

½ cucumber

PREPARATION

Juice all of the ingredients, pour into a glass, and drink immediately.

FACE THE DAY

INGREDIENTS

1 large apple

2 medium carrots

1 medium beet

1 (½-inch) knob of ginger

2 mint leaves

slice of lemon for garnish (optional)

PREPARATION

Juice all of the ingredients, making sure to sandwich the mint leaves between the firmer produce so as not to clog the juicer. Pour into a glass, garnish with lemon slice (if using), and drink immediately.

THE HEAD-TO-TOE GLOW

INGREDIENTS

1 large apple

1 large carrot

½ bulb fennel

¼ medium cucumber

1 vitamin E capsule

PREPARATION

Juice the first 4 ingredients and pour into a glass. Pierce the vitamin E capsule and squeeze into the drink; stir to combine. Drink immediately.

THE SWEET GREEEN

INGREDIENTS

2 medium apples, quartered

2 medium carrots

1 (1-inch) knob of ginger

4 small asparagus spears

¼ cup flat-leaf parsley

¼ cup freshly cut wheatgrass (or 1 tsp. of powdered greens, such as wheatgrass, chlorella, or spirulina)

PREPARATION

Juice the first 5 ingredients and pour into a glass. Add the wheatgrass or powdered greens and stir to combine. Drink immediately.

PURPLE SMASH

INGREDIENTS

2 large apples, quartered

1 cup seedless black grapes

1 cup blueberries, blackberries, or pitted dark cherries

1 tsp. chia seeds

½ Tbsp. cold-pressed flaxseed or olive oil

PREPARATION

Juice the first 3 ingredients and pour into a glass. Stir in the chia seeds and oil; drink immediately.

Juicy Fact

• Chia seeds are considered natural energy boosters—and rightfully so. They are a concentrated food containing healthy omega-3 fatty acids, carbohydrates, protein, fiber, antioxidants, and calcium. When added to a liquid, chia seeds expand, become gelatinous, and can act as a thickening agent. It can be off-putting to some, so it's wise to consume your juice immediately after adding the chia seeds.

CLEAR COMPLEXION

INGREDIENTS

2 Granny Smith (green) apples

¼ small pineapple, peeled, cored, and quartered

½ cucumber

PREPARATION

Juice all of the ingredients, pour into a glass, and drink immediately.

THE CARROT SPRING CLEAN

INGREDIENTS

4 large carrots

2 cup spinach leaves

1 small apple, quartered

1 cup flat-leaf parsley

PREPARATION

Juice all of the ingredients, making sure to alternate between the leafy greens and the firmer produce so as not to clog the juicer. Pour into a glass and drink immediately.

UP THE ANTI(OXIDANTS)

INGREDIENTS

½ cup romaine lettuce

2 tomatoes

1 celery stalk

1 medium carrot

1 scallion

½ cucumber, plus more slices for garnish

1 (½-inch) knob of ginger

PREPARATION

Juice all of the ingredients, making sure to alternate between the softer and firmer produce so as not to clog the juicer. Pour into a glass and drink immediately.

ZUCCHINI BIKINI JUICE

INGREDIENTS

3 cup spinach leaves

2 apples, quartered

1 large zucchini

1 cup romaine lettuce

1 tsp. spirulina or
wheatgrass powder

crushed ice

PREPARATION

Juice the first 4 ingredients, making sure to alternate between the soft and firm produce so as not to clog the juicer.
Pour into a glass and stir in the powdered greens; drink immediately.

PAPAYA POWER

INGREDIENTS

½ papaya, peeled, seeded, and roughly chopped

5 apricots, pitted

2 oranges, peeled

1 lime

¼ cup chilled mineral water

crushed ice

PREPARATION

Juice the first 4 ingredients and pour into an ice–filled glass. Stir in water and drink immediately.

Mocktails

THE PEPPY PINEAPPLE

INGREDIENTS

⅓ large pineapple, peeled, cored, and quartered

1 cucumber

2 large kale leaves, center rib removed

1 medium banana

chilled mineral water, if needed to thin out juice

PREPARATION

Juice the first 3 ingredients, making sure to alternate between the kale and the firmer produce so as not to clog the juicer. In a blender, add the juice and the banana and process until smooth. Add the mineral water (if using), pour into a glass, and drink immediately.

CRAN-ORANGE GINGERTINI

INGREDIENTS

2 cup frozen cranberries, thawed

2 oranges, peeled

crushed ice

2 Tbsp. ginger syrup

½ cup seltzer water, chilled

pomegranate seeds for garnish

PREPARATION

Juice the first 2 ingredients and pour into an ice–filled glass. Stir in ginger syrup and seltzer water; garnish with pomegranate seeds. Drink immediately.

• To make ginger syrup, add 3 cups of coarsely chopped fresh ginger (do not peel) and 1 cup of sugar to 3 cups of water in a medium saucepan. Boil over high heat until ginger is tender and water is a dark amber color (15–20 minutes). Using a colander, strain liquid into a heatproof bottle or other container; chill in the refrigerator before use.

* This recipe makes much more ginger syrup than is needed for the above juice; leftovers can be stored in an airtight bottle in the refrigerator for up to 2 weeks.

CANTALOUPE COOLATA

INGREDIENTS

½ small cantaloupe, peeled and thickly sliced

⅓ small pineapple, peeled, cored, and quartered

2 medium carrots

1 large apple, quartered

crushed ice

PREPARATION

Juice all of the ingredients, pour into an ice-filled glass, and drink immediately.

LIME COLADA

INGREDIENTS

½ pineapple, peeled, cored, and quartered

3 small limes

6 oz. canned coconut milk

crushed ice

lime rind ribbon or pineapple wedge for garnish

PREPARATION

Combine all ingredients in a blender and process until smooth. Pour into a tall glass and garnish with lime rind or pineapple wedge. Drink immediately.

TROPICAL THUNDER

INGREDIENTS

⅓ small pineapple, peeled, cored, and quartered

1 red papaya, peeled, seeded, and roughly chopped

¼ cup guava nectar

extra slices of fruit for garnish

PREPARATION

Juice the first 2 ingredients and pour into a glass. Stir in guava nectar and garnish with extra fruit. Drink immediately.

- Guava nectar can be found in specialty markets (especially Hispanic markets) or in the ethnic foods aisle of traditional grocery stores.

YOU'RE A PEACH

INGREDIENTS

2 large peaches, pitted and halved

2 tangerines, peeled

¾ cup

crushed ice

½ cup seltzer water

PREPARATION

Juice the first 3 ingredients and pour into an ice–filled glass. Stir in seltzer water and drink immediately.

STRAWBERRY SURPRISE

INGREDIENTS

10 large strawberries

½ cucumber

1 large apple, cored

2 medium carrots

PREPARATION

Juice all of the ingredients, pour into a glass, and drink immediately.

ORANGE CRUSH

INGREDIENTS

4 tangerines, peeled

½ ruby red grapefruit

1 cup strawberries

1 apple

¼ cucumber

crushed ice

PREPARATION

Juice all of the ingredients, pour into an ice–filled glass, and drink immediately.

KNOCK-YOU-NAKED JUICE

INGREDIENTS

3 large nectarines, pitted and halved

2 apples, quartered

1 orange, peeled

1 cup ginger ale

2 Tbsp. pomegranate seeds

PREPARATION

Juice the first 3 ingredients and pour into a glass. Stir in the ginger ale and garnish with the pomegranate seeds. Drink immediately.

Juicy Fact

• To make ginger ale, first make a ginger syrup by adding 3 cups of coarsely chopped fresh ginger (do not peel) and 1 cup of sugar to 3 cups of water in a medium saucepan. Boil over high heat until ginger is tender and water is a dark amber color (15–20 minutes). Using a colander, strain liquid into a heatproof bottle or other container; chill in the refrigerator before use. Add 1 cup of ginger syrup to 1 cup of club soda and pour into an airtight bottle.

*This recipe makes much more ginger syrup than needed for the ginger ale recipe; leftovers can be stored in an airtight bottle in the refrigerator for up to 2 weeks.

THE YULE MULE

INGREDIENTS

6 clementines

2 figs, halved

2 apples, cored

1 orange

½ cup frozen cranberries, thawed

1 (½-inch) knob of ginger

extra slices of fruit, for garnish

1 piece star anise, 3 whole cloves, or 1 cinnamon stick (if serving warm)

PREPARATION

Juice all of the ingredients and pour into a glass. Garnish with extra fruit and drink immediately. If serving warm, add star anise, cloves, or cinnamon.

Notes

Notes

About the Author

IRIS McCARTHY is the only Yankee in a family of Southerners—all of whom know their way around a kitchen. Refusing to allow her birthplace to keep her from her culinary pursuits, Iris credits her mother with teaching her the difference between a whisk and a spatula. Currently, she enjoys a food writing career that allows her to hold a pen in one hand and an egg beater in the other. On most days, you can find Iris making delicious messes in the kitchen and writing about it on her popular website www.thepalateprincess.com.